Team Batman

by Beth Davies

Batman created by Bob Kane with Bill Finger

Editor Pamela Afram
Designer Sam Bartlett
Senior Editor Hannah Dolan
Senior Designer Nathan Martin
Pre-production Producer Siu Yin Chan
Producer Louise Daly
Managing Editor Paula Regan
Design Managers Guy Harvey and Jo Connor
Publisher Julie Ferris
Art Director Lisa Lanzarini
Publishing Director Simon Beecroft

Batman created by Bob Kane with Bill Finger

First American Edition, 2017
Published in the United States by DK Publishing
345 Hudson Street, New York, New York 10014

Page design copyright © 2017 Dorling Kindersley Limited
DK, a Division of Penguin Random House LLC
17 18 19 20 10 9 8 7 6 5 4 3 2 1

001–297919–Jan/2017

Page design Copyright ©2017 Dorling Kindersley Limited

A catalog record for this book is available from the Library of Congress.

ISBN 978-1-4654-5860-5 (Hardcover)
ISBN 978-1-4654-5859-9 (Paperback)

DK books are available at special discounts when purchased in bulk for sales
promotions, premiums, fund-raising, or educational use. For details, contact:
DK Publishing Special Markets, 345 Hudson Street, New York, New York 10014
SpecialSales@dk.com

Printed and bound in the USA

A WORLD OF IDEAS:
SEE ALL THERE IS TO KNOW

www.dk.com
www.LEGO.com

Contents

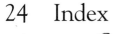

Batman

Batman is a super hero.
His job is to catch villains
and keep Gotham City safe.
Batman does not usually want
anyone else to help him.
He likes to work alone.

Gotham City

Batman lives in Gotham City.
The city is full of mean villains.
Sometimes, Batman cannot
catch all of the bad guys.
Maybe Batman needs help
from his friends.

Robin

Robin is a young boy
whom Batman adopted.
Robin wants to help
his new dad on his
awesome missions.
Batman's butler, Alfred,
is happy Batman has
someone to work with.
Alfred thinks he spends
too much time alone.

Batgirl

Batgirl wants to catch villains
in Gotham City, too.
She thinks being part of
a team is best.
She wants to help Batman.
Batman is not sure about this.
He likes to work alone!

REAL NAMES

Nobody knows who Batman is under his mask.
When he is not fighting crime, Batman looks
just like everyone else.
He even has a different name.
Batgirl and Robin also have different names.
Don't tell anyone!

BATMAN

Real name:
Bruce Wayne

Job:
Rich businessman

Likes:
Lobster dinners,
stylish suits, parties

BATGIRL

Real name:
Barbara Gordon

Job:
Commissioner of
Gotham City Police
Department

Likes:
Teamwork, catching
criminals, flying planes

ROBIN

Real name:
Dick Grayson

Job:
Being helpful

Likes:
Batman, having
a family, capes

The Scuttler

Batman loves cool vehicles.
Alfred helps him build them.
This is the Scuttler.
It is shaped like a bat.
It has lots of gadgets.

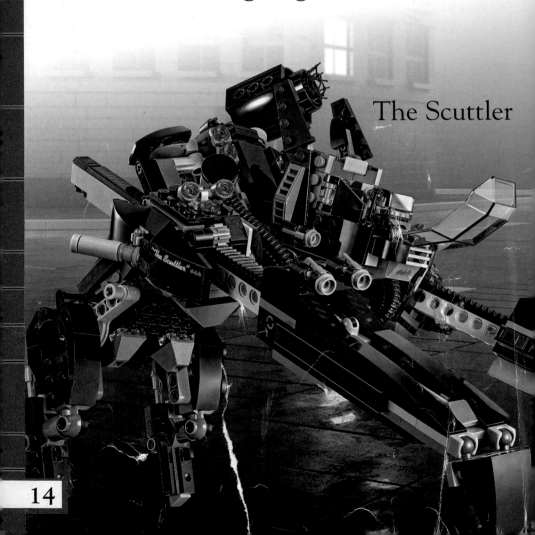

The Scuttler

The Batmobile is built in
Batman's favorite color: black.
Batman adds a second seat for
Robin to sit in.

The Batmobile

The Rogues

The Joker is Batman's enemy.
He wants to take over
Gotham City.

The Joker has a team of villains
who help him cause trouble.
The terrible team is called
the Rogues.

Teamwork

Batman needs to battle the
Rogues in Gotham City.
He asks Robin and Batgirl for
help. Robin leaps at Man-Bat.

Batgirl chases Harley Quinn.
Watch out for Mr. Freeze's
freeze gun, Batgirl!
Batman catches the Joker.
Great work, team!

Quiz

1. What is Batman's favorite color?

2. Who is Robin's new dad?

3. What is the team of villains called?

4. Which villain carries a freeze gun?

5. What is Batgirl's real name?

6. Who is the Joker's enemy?

7. What animal is the Scuttler shaped like?

Answers on page 22

Glossary

butler

A servant who looks after a wealthy person's house.

enemy

A person who does not want to be friendly.

gadget

An object that is very useful for a specific job.

mission

A special task to complete.

vehicle

Something that transports people or objects.

villain

A person who likes to cause trouble.

A Note to Parents

THIS BOOK is part of an exciting four-level reading series for children, developing the habit of reading widely for both pleasure and information. The series is designed in conjunction with leading literacy experts, including Dr. Linda Gambrell, Distinguished Professor of Education at Clemson University. Dr. Gambrell has served as President of the National Reading Conference, the College Reading Association, and the International Reading Association.

Beautiful illustrations and superb full-color photographs combine with engaging, easy-to-read stories to offer a fresh approach to each subject in the series. Each DK Reader is guaranteed to capture a child's interest while developing his or her reading skills, general knowledge and love of reading.

The four levels of reading books are aimed at different reading abilities, enabling you to choose the books that are exactly right for your child:

Level 1: Learning to read
Level 2: Beginning to read
Level 3: Beginning to read alone
Level 4: Reading alone

The "normal" age at which a child begins to read can be anywhere from three to eight years old. Adult participation through the lower levels is very helpful for providing encouragement, discussing storylines, and sounding out unfamiliar words.

No matter which level you select, you can be sure that you are helping your child learn to read, then read to learn!

Index